Brilliant Support Activities

Understanding Living Things

Janet O'Neill,
Alan Jones
Roy Purnell

Brilliant
PUBLICATIONS

We hope you and your class enjoy using this book. Other books in the series include:

Understanding Materials
printed ISBN: 978-1-78317-096-8
ebook ISBN: 978-1-78317-100-2

Understanding Light, Sound and Forces
printed ISBN: 978-1-78317-097-5
ebook ISBN: 978-1-78317-101-9

Published by Brilliant Publications
Unit 10
Sparrow Hall Farm
Edlesborough
Dunstable
Bedfordshire
LU6 2ES, UK

E-mail: info@brilliantpublications.co.uk
Website: www.brilliantpublications.co.uk
Tel: 01525 222292

The name Brilliant Publications and the logo are registered trademarks.

Written by Janet O'Neill, Alan Jones and Roy Purnell

Designed and illustrated by Small World Design

The authors are grateful to the staff and pupils of Gellideg Junior School, Merthyr Tydfil for their help.

© Text: Janet O'Neill, Alan Jones and
   Roy Purnell

Printed ISBN: 978-1-78317-095-1
Ebook ISBN: 978-1-78317-099-9

First printed and published in the UK in 2014

10 9 8 7 6 5 4 3 2 1

Contents

© Janet O'Neill, Alan Jones and Roy Purnell

Introduction to Everyday Living Things

This book shows the relevance and importance of understanding the science of everyday Living Things.

It is NOT a complete textbook on all aspects of the area of Everyday Biology, plants and animals.

This series of three books is designed to help the slower learner or pupils with various learning difficulties operating at the lower levels of understanding at KS1 and KS2 (even though they might be at an older physical age). The activities of this book follows the areas of science outlined in the Programmes of Study of the Science National Curriculum for years 1–3 and selected topics of years 4 and 5. The biology topics cover a wide range of familiar and commonly encountered concepts. They are divided in this book according to the headings of the National Curriculum and grouped in activities related to Plants followed by Living Things (animals and humans).

The activities should help to develop the essential Scientific Enquiry skills as indiated in the POS of the National Curriculum namely those of 'Observation', 'Predicting', Recording', and 'Drawing Conclusions' through the activities included in the book.

The books contain a mixture of paper-based tasks and also some 'hands on' activities. The following symbols on each sheet have been used to indicate the type of activities.

 What to do

 Think and do

 Read

 Investigate

The sheets involving practical investigations use materials readily available in most schools or homes. The activities have been vetted for safety, but, as with any classroom based activity, it is the responsibility of the classroom teacher to do a risk assessment with their pupils in mind.

The sheets generally introduce one concept area per sheet. They are designed to be used by single pupils or as a classroom activity if all the pupils are working in the same ability range. Alternatively they can be used as a separate sheet for slower learners working on the same topic as the rest of the class, hence helping differentiation within the topic area. The sheets are easily modified for specific pupils or groups. They can be used in any suitable order as there is no hierachy with the sequence in the books. They can also be useful for home tuition or for the pupils to do if they are in hospitals or prolonged home stay.

The sheets can be used for assessment purposes or homework tasks.

Generally the sheets can be used with older pupils if they are operating within the expectations and understanding level comensurate with pupils at KS1 and KS2. The sheets use simple language and clear black line illustrations to make them easy to read without colour distractions. They have reduced number of words and a straight forward vocabulary to help poor readers or pupils whose language skills might be limited. Written responses are required so helping writing and communication skills of pupils. The completion of the sheets can be done by a support teacher responding to a verbal or a sign instruction by the pupil. It is essential that all pupils feel a sense of success and achievement when doing science as it is part of their everyday life.

No particular reference has been made to any specific type of learning difficulty or disability as the material has been successfully tested with a wide range of pupils. The teachers modify the method of use as the sheets can be enlarged or the instructions read onto a sound disc or computer. The sheets are easily converted to be shown on larger screens or computer screens.

The topics of this book match the New (and old) National Curriculum and cover the areas of 'Everyday Living Things' and help the pupils use the various processes and methods of science.

The worksheets in this book sometimes overlap with other activities but this will help the pupils to grasp the concepts in a different context. Some topics also take ideas from another science area just to show the links between the everyday science we use. The worksheets can be used in any suitable sequence as this is not a logical teaching scheme. They are designed to give flexibility and diversity to teachers with pupils working with a wide range of abilities within a class. Some topics have been chosen that are from the POS of year 4 to 6 but written with the slower pupils in mind. Other topics can be linked with geography, eg weather and environments. Any numeracy work is at the lower levels of expectancy.

Some sheets encourage direct answers to specific questions whereas other activities require some degree of thinking before making a written response. The symbols on the sheets give an indication of this. The questions and presentation are simple but the level of answers often reveal higher levels of understanding than expected.

The pupils will probably be more familiar with the contents of this book than the other two in the series so any activities and questions can be extended to push the pupils to their highest level of knowledge. Many will be experts in the areas to do with animals due to them having pets, other pupils will be plant growers and their knowledge can be shared with others during an activity. Whenever possible allow the pupils to do a practical activity associated with the worksheet.

National Curriculum POS and the Activities of this book
Because the New NC does not clearly indicate separate statements of the POS by using a nomenclature of numbering or letters within any areas it has been found convenient for OUR books to code and summarize these main sections of the NC. This will help the teacher see how the topics covered in this, and the other books in the series, cover the POS of the National Curriculum. They are all covered by the activities, some more than once.

New National Curriclum

Letter headings are ours but refer to the NC statements quoted on the pages of NC

Processes needing to be covered:	Content of the POS
KS1 Our Summary of POS which are appropriate for Pupils both in Year 1 and 2, 'Working Scientifically', (WS) p 139 NC WSa Asking questions, and answering WSb Observing and using simple euipment WSc Testing ideas WSd Identifying and Classifying WSe Using observations to suggest answers WSf Gathering data to answer question	**KS1 Our Summary of POS for Year 1 'Everyday Biology', (B) p 140 & 141 of NC,** B1 Common plants and animals B2 Structure of common flowering plants B3 Identifying common animals, birds, fish B4 What animals eat B5 Structure of common animals, all types B6 Identify and name parts of human body
Working Scientifically POS page149 National Curriculum. KS1, Year 1 and Lower KS2 The skils and POS used in Year 3 and Year 4 need to be adapted for the slower learning pupils but they are generally an extension of the skills of WSa to WSf above	**KS1, Our Summary of POS for Year 2 Everday Biology page144 NC** B7 Living and dead things B8 Habitats B9 Names of plants, animals in their habitats B10 Foods for animals and simple food chains B11 Seeds and Bulbs B12 What plants need to grow B13 Animal babies grow to adults B14 Basic needs of animals and humans and survival B15 Diets and hygiene
Relevant sections of Year 4 Page 155 NC The POS of Year 4 and Year 5 are more detailed and in depth studies of what has gone before and might need to be referred to but are generally outside the needs of the slower learner	**Lower KS2 Our Summary of POS for Year 3 and Year 4 see page 151 NC** B16 Functions of parts of plants B17 Exploring the specific needs of different plants B18 Transportation of water in plants B19 Flowers and life cycle of plants B20 Right type of food for animals and humans B21 Humans and animals have skeletons and muscles for purpose

Brilliant Support Activities **Understanding Living Things**

Links to the National Curriculum

Page Number	Title of Activity	National Curriculum Working Scientifically, (WS)	National Curriculum Everyday Biology (B)
	Plants		
8	Growing plants 1	a,b,c,e,f	B 1,11,12
9	Growing plants 2	a,b,c,e,f	B 1,11,12,18
10	Dying plants	a,b,c,e	B 11,12,19
11	Plants in the old	a,b,c,e,f	B 2,11,12,16,17,19
12	Pollination	a,b,c,e,f	B 12,16
13	Seeds 1	a,b,c,e	B 11
14	Seeds 2	a,b,c	B 11,12,16
15	Different plants	a,b,d,f	B 1,2,11
16	Changes in a tree	a,b,d,e,f	B 16,19
17	Plants live here	a,e,f	B 1,8,9
18	Environment	a,b,f	B 8,9
	Living Things, Animals, and Humans		
19	Living things	a,b,d,e,f	B 1,7
20	Living and non living	a,c	B 7
21	Alive and not alive	a,b,d,e,f	B 7
22	Where fish live	a,e,f	B 3,8,9
23	Where do I live?	a,c,d,e,f	B 1,8,9
24	Some animals eat other animals	a,c,e	B 10,14
25	Food chains	a,c,e,f	B 4,10
26	What animal?	a,b,d,e,f	B 1,3,5
27	Making keys	f	B 3
28	Frog cycle	a,b,c,e,f	B 13
29	Mini-beast families	a,b,c	B 1,13
30	Guessing animals	a,c,d,f	B 1,3,5
31	Growing up	a,d	B 5,13
32	Bones, bones, bones	a,b,c,d,e	B 5, 21
33	Skeletons	a,b,c,e	B 1,5,21
34	Muscles	a,b,c,e	B 1,5,21
35	Teeth	a,b,c,d,e	B 4,5,6
36	Food for life	a,c,e,f	B 4,10,15
37	Good food	a,c,d,e,f	B 4,10,15
38	Pulse	a,b,c,e,f	B 5,21
39	The heart of the matter	a,b,c,e,f	B 1,5,6,22
40	Heart	a,b,c,e	B 5,6,14,15,20
41	Blood	a,b,c,e,f	B 5,6,14,15,20
42	The body	a,b,c,d,f	B 5,6,14,15,20
43	Excercise	a,b,d,e,f	B 4,5,7,10,15
44	Healthy living	a,b,d,e,f	B 4,14,15,20
45	Staying healthy	a,b,c,e	B 4,10,14,20
46	Unhealthy living	a,b,c,e	B 4,7,14,15,20
47	Diseases	a,b,c,f	B 15
48	Micro-organisms	a,b,c,e,f	B 16 and Yr 4 POS

What to do

Paul has some tomato seeds. He wants to grow tomatoes.
He wants to sell them to make some money.

Use these words to complete the sentences:

seeds	pot	soil
sunny place	water	label

1. Paul put the **s** _ _ _ in the **p** _ _ .

2. Then he added the **s** _ _ _ _ .

3. He added **w** _ _ _ _ .

4. He put a **l** _ _ _ _ on the pot.

5. Then he placed the pot in a **s** _ _ _ _ _ **p** _ _ _ _ _ .

Think and do

What would happen if the seeds were not watered often? . . . .
. . . .

What would happen if the pot was put in a dark place? . . . .
. . . .

You could also investigate this at home.

What to do

Name the parts of the plant.

Draw lines from the names to the plant.

leaves   **flower**   **roots**   **stem**

f . . . .

l . . . .

s . . . .

r . . . .

Work out the missing words:

Plants need water to live.

Plants take up water from the soil using their **r** __ __ __ __.
The stem carries the water from the roots to the **l** __ __ __ __ __ .
The **f** __ __ __ __ __ __ makes seeds.

Think and do

Can a plant grow well in the dark?   Yes ☐   No ☐
What does the flower attract? Sort out the letters:
       i c t s e n s   i __ __ __ __ __ __

Why do some plants attract bees?. . . . .

The leaves need **S** __ __ /**L** __ __ __ __ __ to help the plant to grow.

Dying plants

What to do
Here are some plants.

1. Water
No plant food
Sunlight

2. No water
Plant food
Sunlight

3. Water
Plant food
Grown in the dark

4. Water
Plant food
Sunlight

  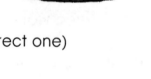

Which do you think will grow the best? **1 2 3 4** (Circle the correct one)

Why will the rest not grow so well? . . . .

. . . .
You could investigate this.

Think and do
A plant will not grow on the moon's surface because

. . . .

. . . .

© Janet O'Neill, Alan Jones and Roy Purnell

Plants in the cold

Read
A seed that starts to grow is **germinating.**

What to do
Which seed will germinate quickest if watered? . . . .

1. Seed in soil in a refrigerator

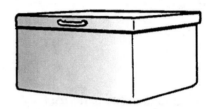

2. Seed in soil in a deep freeze

3. Seed in soil outside in winter

4. Seed in soil in a warm house

You could investigate this.

To start a seed growing, you must have . . . . and . . . .

Think and do
Place a pea or bean seed on some wet cotton wool in the classroom. Leave it for a week or so and keep the cotton wool wet. Draw what happens.

What would happen if a similar experiment was done in a dark cupboard?

. . . .

What to do

Draw lines from the labels to the plant:

Leaves

Petals

Where pollen is found

Where seeds are formed

How do insects and bees help **pollination**?

. . . .

. . . .

Draw on the flower where the bee goes for pollen.

What does the bee do with the pollen?

. . . .

. . . .

Think and do

Pollination is needed because ...

. . . .

Seeds, 1

What to do

Some plants reproduce by making seeds.

Draw how a tomato plant grows from seed.

1. Seed planting

2. Seed sprouting

3. Young plant growing

4. Tomatoes forming

Think and do

How can the ripe tomatoes be used to grow other new tomato plants? . . . .

. . . .

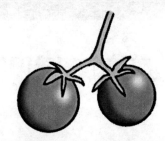

What to do

Seeds need to be **dispersed** or moved to another place.

Draw lines to show what helps the seeds to be moved. (You can draw more than one line to each plant.)

Dandelion

Wind blows

Horse chestnut (conker)

Squirrels

Blackberry

Birds

Weed seeds

Humans

Oak acorns

Apples

Think and do

Why do the seeds need to be moved to another place?

. . . .

Different plants

What to do

The words in bold print are mixed up.
Write out what the words should be.

Surface of the water

Seaweed

Bubbles of air

Seaweed uses the air sacks to help it **tolaf** to the surface to get **nus thigl.**

. . . .

. . . .

The ivy clings to the wall using strong **toors.**

. . . .

. . . .

The sweet pea uses a twisting stem to help it **dants pu.**

. . . .

. . . .

Think and do

How do runner beans grow up a stick and hold on?

. . . .

. . . .

. . . .

What to do

A tree changes during the year.
The pictures show how an apple tree changes from spring to autumn.

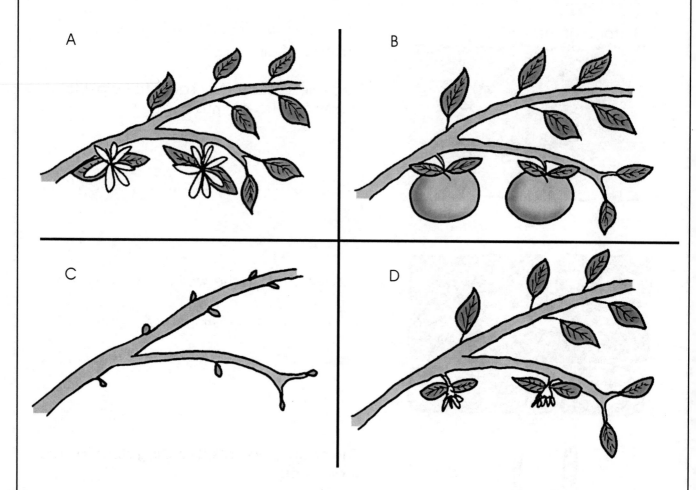

A

B

C

D

Put the letters in order in the boxes to show how the apple tree changes.
The first is done.

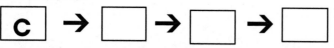

At what time of year do you see picture C?   S _ _ _ _ _

Think and do

What season comes next after spring?   S _ _ _ _ _

What season comes next after summer? . . . .

Where do you find the seeds of an apple? . . . .

Plants live here

What to do

Draw lines to show where you think the plants grow best. It is called their habitat.

Heather

Lichen

Seaweed

Wheat

House plant

Think and do

Different plants like to live in different places.

A house plant will NOT like to grow __ __ __ __ __ __ __ __ .

Seaweed will NOT grow . . . .

The different places are called the plant's **H __ B __ T __ T**.

Environment

What to do

The whole surrounding area that plants, animals or something lives in is called their environment.

The area around the school needs to be kept clean to make a good environment. Why?

Write or draw about each picture's environment.

trees

. . . .

. . . .

. . . .

rubbish

. . . .

. . . .

. . . .

cars and buses

. . . .

. . . .

animal/bird waste

. . . .

. . . .

. . . .

Think and do

How does neglecting the environment affect people's health?

. . . .

. . . .

Is the area of your school a healthy environment? . . . .

© Janet O'Neill, Alan Jones and Roy Purnell

What to do

Put a tick ✓ by things that all living things do to keep alive.

Need food ☐

Reproduce ☐

Need water ☐

Like music ☐

Need light ☐

Grow ☐

Move ☐

Watch television ☐

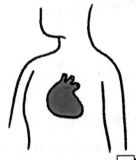

Keep clean and healthy ☐

Think and do

Animals have blood which takes the food around the body.

What do plants have that does this? . . . .

Living and non-living

What to do

The place where living things are found (their home) is called their habitat.
Put a tick ✓ by the things that are alive now.

Tree ☐

Flower ☐

Corn flakes ☐

Rocks ☐

Butterfly ☐

Bird ☐

Mouse ☐

Wooden pencil ☐

Worm ☐

Could all the living things here live in the same field? Yes/No

This is called their **H __ B __ T __ T .**

Think and do

Draw a ring round the things that all living things need to stay alive.

Water   TV   Food   Phone   Holidays   Air   Car   Light

Alive and not alive

What to do

Some of the things below are alive. Some are not alive.

Grass

Water

Flower

Slug

Cloud

Crab

Rain

The Sun

Toothbrush

Put the words in the correct list:

Alive

....
....
....
....
....
....

Not alive

....
....
....
....
....
....

Where fish live

What to do
Fish live and swim under water.

Draw lines from the words to the parts of the fish.

Eye   Tail

Fins   Gills

Mouth

Which things help the fish move through the water?

. . . .

. . . .

Fish use **g** _ _ _ _ to breathe under water.

Think and do
Describe how the fish breathes the air dissolved in the water

. . . .

. . . .

Can whales (mammals) breathe under water? . . . .

© Janet O'Neill, Alan Jones and Roy Purnell

Where do I live?

What to do
Where would you expect me to live? What is my habitat?

Draw lines.

Dog

Mouse

Rabbit

Cow

Sparrow

Think and do
Different animals live in different places because . . . .

. . . .

The place close to where an animal lives is called its **H __ B __ T __ T .**

Some animals eat other animals

Read

Birds eat snails.

Snails eat leaves.

Slugs eat leaves.

Sparrow hawks eat small birds.

Birds eat slugs.

What to do

Give an example of one animal eating another animal.

Animals that eats other animals are called **C _ R _ I _ O _ E S .**

Name one enemy of small birds . . . .

Show two food chains, starting from a plant

. . . .

. . . .

. . . .

Animals that eat both plants and animals are called omnivores. Are humans carnivores, herbivores or omnivores?

. . . .

Food chains

Read

A cow eats grass → A cow makes milk → I drink milk

The illustration above describes a **food chain.** Food chains nearly always start with a green plant.

What to do

A dog eats dog food made from beef. Draw the food chain, starting with grass.

grass →

A cat eats 'Catto-fish' cat food. Draw this food chain, starting with plankton in the sea.

plankton or seaweed →

Jamie likes to eat hamburgers. Draw the food chain.

grass →

Think and do

Use another sheet of paper to draw the food chain of a sparrow hawk, starting with a cabbage leaf.

cabbage leaf →

What to do

A

B

C

D

E

Use the key to identify the animals.

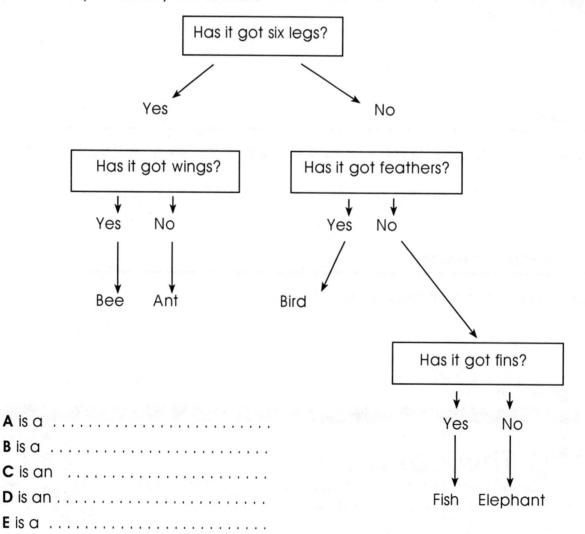

Has it got six legs?

Yes

No

Has it got wings?

Has it got feathers?

Yes   No

Yes   No

Bee   Ant

Bird

Has it got fins?

Yes   No

Fish   Elephant

A is a . . . .

B is a . . . .

C is an . . . .

D is an . . . .

E is a . . . .

Brilliant Support Activities **Understanding Living Things**

© Janet O'Neill, Alan Jones and Roy Purnell

What to do

When you make a key you must ask questions that can be answered by **yes** or **no**.

Look at the key for sorting out coins.

| 50p | 1p | 2p | 5p | 20p | £1 | £2 |

There is no right or wrong way to sort them out. You can make your own yes/no questions.

Work out where the coins should go.

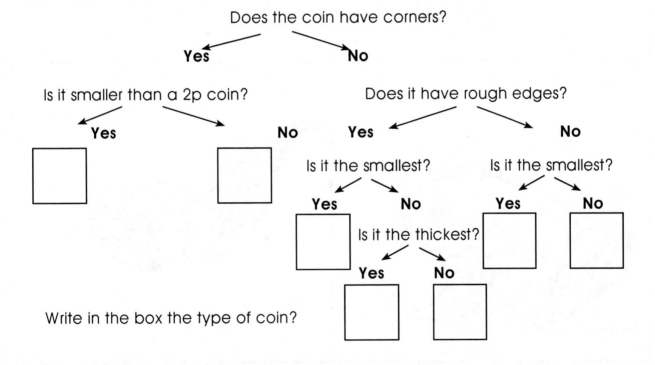

Does the coin have corners?

Yes — No

Is it smaller than a 2p coin?

Yes — No

Does it have rough edges?

Yes — No

Is it the smallest?

Yes — No

Is it the smallest?

Yes — No

Is it the thickest?

Yes — No

Write in the box the type of coin?

Think and do

Joe found these leaves in the garden. Make a key to help him sort them.

Holly   Horse chestnut   Oak   Apple   Maple

What to do

Put these pictures in order of their life cycle. Start with the eggs.

1. (   ) ⟶ 2. (   ) ⟶ 3. (   ) ⟶ 4. (   )

A

B

C

D

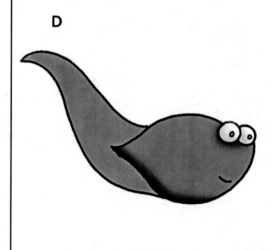

Think and do

What do frogs like to eat?

. . . .

Who lays the eggs – the male or female frog?. . . . .

. . . .

Mini-beast families

What to do

Kelly was in the woods and she saw some mini-beasts.
She put them into two groups.

Group 1

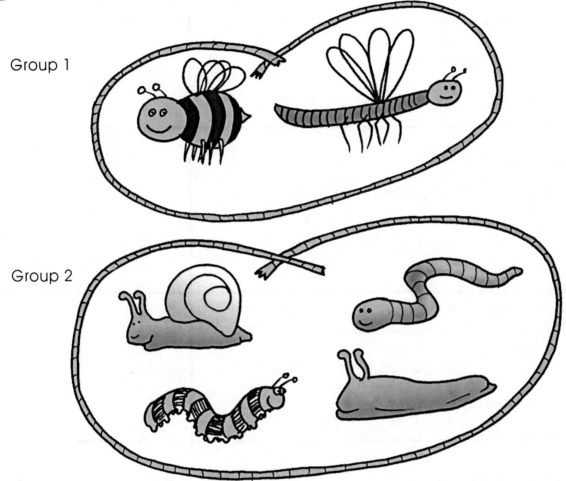

Group 2

How can the mini-beasts in group 1 move ? . . . .

How do mini-beasts in group 2 move? . . . .

Suppose Kelly found a house fly. Which group would it be in? . . . .

Think and do

Why is it helpful to put mini-beasts into different groups?

. . . .

Can you name one of the mini-beasts in each group? . . . .

. . . .

Guessing animals

What to do
Read these sentences. Guess the living things. Draw a picture of each one.

I walk on four legs.
I have a long tail.
I purr when someone strokes me.

I am a **c** . . . .

I grow on a tall plant.
I am a vegetable.
Sometimes people call me a 'runner'.

I am a **b** . . . .

I cannot see very well as I live underground.
People do not like to pick me up as they say
I am slippery.
I might live in your garden or in a field.

I am a **w** . . . .

I have a bushy tail.
I love to gather nuts and hide them for the winter.
I sleep most of the winter in a secret hideout.

I am a **s** . . . .

Think and do
Make up a few sentences of your own about a plant or animal living near you but don't give away its name.

. . . .

. . . .

Test your friends to see if they can guess what it is called.

Brilliant Support Activities **Understanding Living Things**

© Janet O'Neill, Alan Jones and Roy Purnell

What to do

As we grow older our bodies change.
Write the words next to the correct pictures:

baby   **teenager**   **girl**   **toddler**

boy   **adult**   **old age**

b _ _ _   t _ _ _ _ _ _ _   g _ _ _

t _ _ _ _ _ _ _   b _ _

o _ _ _ _ _   a _ _ _ _

Write the names in order, start with the youngest.

Think and do

At what age do you become a teenager?   _____ years

How old are you in your last year of being a teenager? _____ years

At what age do people get state pensions?   _____ years

Bones, bones, bones

What to do

Sort the letters to find the parts of the body.
Draw lines from the words to the correct parts of the body.

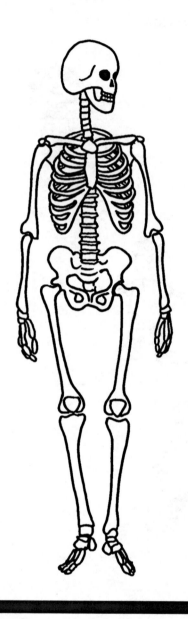

The bone of the head
is a **sullk.** . . . .

The bones of the chest
are **birs.** . . . .

The bone that holds the body
up is the **cabk** bone. . . . .

The leg bends at the
keen. . . . .

Label any other bones you
know.

What is the purpose of the spine?

. . . .

. . . .

. . . .

Think and do

Fill in the missing words:

Our brain is inside the **s** . . . .

The skeleton is made of **b** . . . .

Colour in the **pelvis** on the picture.

Brilliant Support Activities **Understanding Living Things**

© Janet O'Neill, Alan Jones and Roy Purnell

Skeletons

What to do

Put a tick ✓ in the correct box for each picture.

Kangaroo

Does it have a skeleton? Yes ☐ No ☐

Slug

Does it have a skeleton? Yes ☐ No ☐

Baby

Does it have a skeleton? Yes ☐ No ☐

Bird

Does it have a skeleton? Yes ☐ No ☐

Fish

Does it have a skeleton? Yes ☐ No ☐

Frog

Does it have a skeleton? Yes ☐ No ☐

Think and do

Why do we have skeletons?

. . . .

Do jelly fish have skeletons? . . . .

Muscles

What to do

Fred wants to be able to pick up heavy weights.

What does he need to build up?

Cross out the incorrect words.

hair/muscles/bones

Jo wants to throw the ball further.
Which muscles does she need to strengthen?

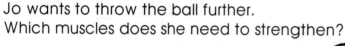

Which muscles does Ranjit use when he kicks the ball?

After exercising a lot, what aches?

Cross out the incorrect words.

bones/blood/muscles

Think and do

List the muscles you use most during the day.

. . . .

What happens to muscles if you don't use them?

. . . .

Brilliant Support Activities **Understanding Living Things**

© Janet O'Neill, Alan Jones and Roy Purnell

Teeth

What to do

Look at this picture of teeth in your mouth.

Draw lines from the labels to the tooth picture.

We have three types of teeth: molars
incisors
canines

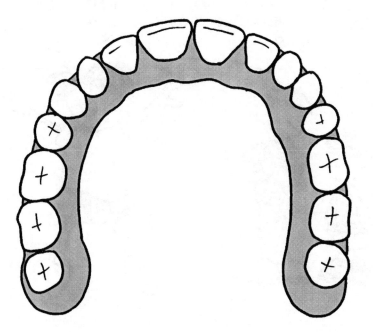

i _ _ _ _ _ _

c _ _ _ _ _

m _ _ _ _

Think and do

Which teeth do we use for biting our food? . . . .

Which teeth do we use for grinding our food? . . . .

What do the other teeth do? . . . .

Food for life

What to do
Work out the missing words.

I eat food to keep me
a _ _ _ _ _

I use food to
give me
e _ _ _ _ _ _

I use food
to help me
stay alive and
g _ _ _ _

I use food
to keep me
h_ _ _ _ _ _ _ _

A car needs fuel to keep going.

F _ _ _   is like the fuel to keep **me** going.

Think and do
My favourite food is ...

It is important to have breakfast before coming to school because . . . .

. . . .

Brilliant Support Activities **Understanding Living Things**

© Janet O'Neill, Alan Jones and Roy Purnell

Good food

Read
You must have a balanced diet of good food to keep healthy.

What to do
Jo and Di had lunch boxes.

crisps

cream cake

chocolate bar

can of coke

apple

cheese

brown bread roll

and salad filling

carton of milk

Who had a well-balanced meal? . . . .

Think and do
Write down what you had for breakfast..

Was it a well balanced meal?   Yes ☐   No ☐

Why? . . . .

Is your favourite food always the best for you? . . . .   Why?

. . . .

Pulse

Read

The heart pumps blood around the body.
It beats about 72 times a minute.

What to do

Work out the missing words:

As the heart pumps, you can hear your **h** _ _ _ _ **b** _ _ _ _ .

You can also feel your pulse.

A doctor uses a **st** _ _ _ _ **scope** to listen to your heart.

Investigate

Make a shape like this with some Blu-tack or Plasticine
and a matchstick.

Put your arm palm upwards on a table.

Put the Blu-tack on the pulse point on
your wrist or on the side of your thumb.

Write or draw what happens.

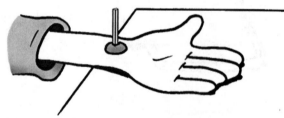

Count how many pulses you have in one minute: . . . .

Think and do

Rob ran around at play time.

Does his pulse rate go up or down?

You could investigate this.

Brilliant Support Activities **Understanding Living Things**

© Janet O'Neill, Alan Jones and Roy Purnell

The heart of the matter

What to do

Draw an arrow to show where your heart is in your body.

How big is your heart?
Put a tick ✓ by the correct answer:

My heart is the size of a   golf ball   ☐

                                 tennis ball   ☐

                                 football   ☐

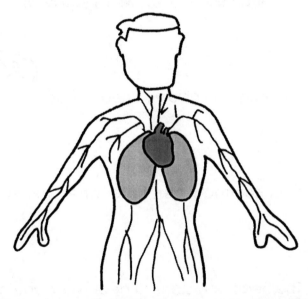

Label the diagram to show how blood goes around in the body.

Veins

Arteries

Heart

Lungs

Think and do

What happens to your heart when you run?

. . . .

What happens to your heart when you go to sleep?

. . . .

Heart

What to do

Put a tick ✓ by the sentences that are correct.

❑ The heart pumps blood around the body.

❑ I feel love with my heart.

❑ The heart slows down when you sleep.

❑ Smoking can give you heart trouble.

❑ Your heartbeat gets faster when you run.

❑ The heart only starts to beat when you are born.

Think and do

Do animals like cats and dogs have hearts?   Yes ❑   No ❑

Do plants have hearts?   Yes ❑   No ❑

Blood

What to do

Put a tick ✓ in the correct box.

Blood is   red. ☐

green. ☐

yellow. ☐

Blood carries

chocolate ☐

oxygen ☐

juice ☐   around the body.

Blood is pumped around the body by the

brain. ☐

lungs. ☐

heart. ☐

How many pints of blood are in an adult body?   2 ☐

7 ☐

10 ☐

Think and do

Do animals like cats and dogs have blood?   Yes ☐   No ☐

Do plants have blood?   Yes ☐   No ☐

Do fish have blood?   Yes ☐   No ☐

What to do

We have things called **organs** inside our bodies.

They are the:

| brain | heart | kidneys | lungs |

Draw lines from the words to the body where the organs are.

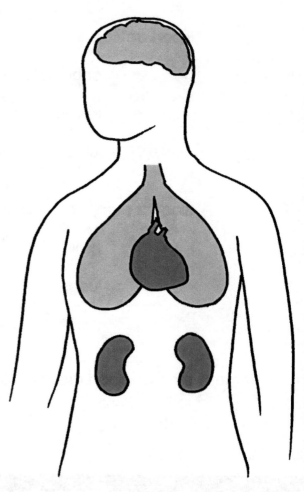

b _ _ _ _

l _ _ _ _

h _ _ _ _

k _ _ _ _ _ _ _

Think and do

Which organ pumps blood around the body? . . . .

Which organ does the thinking? . . . .

What is the job of the kidneys? . . . .

Which organ can take in air? . . . .

Brilliant Support Activities **Understanding Living Things**

© Janet O'Neill, Alan Jones and Roy Purnell

Exercise

What to do

Put a tick ✓ by those things that change when you exercise (like, running fast).

How do they change when you exercise?

	Change?	Say how they change
Breathing		
Blood moving around body		
Heartbeat		
Body temperature		
Your teeth		
Your fitness		
Hair growth		
How tired you are		
Sweating		

Think and do

Why is it good to exercise on a regular basis?

. . . .

What to do

Put a tick ✓ by those things that help good health.

Smoking ☐

Drinking alcohol ☐

Regular exercise ☐

Balanced diet ☐

Eating fruit ☐

Sniffing glue ☐

Eating sweets ☐

Peaceful life ☐

Think and do

Why is smoking bad for you? . . . .

What happens to your body when you become unwell? . . . .

. . . .

Staying healthy

What to do
We wash our hands, to help stop stomach upsets and diseases.

Put these phrases in the correct places.

Eating less sweets	Staying away from cigarette smoke
Coughing into a handkerchief	Regular exercise

C. . . . . helps to stop the spread of colds.

E . . . . helps to stop toothache.

R . . . . helps to keeps you in good health.

S . . . . helps you to stop getting lung cancer.

Think and do
Write three things you do to stay healthy.

1. . . . .

2. . . . .

3. . . . .

Unhealthy living

What to do

Put a cross ✖ by those things that are unhealthy and a tick ✓ for healthy things.

Smoking ☐

Balanced diet ☐

Alcohol ☐

Over eating ☐

Sniffing glue ☐

Polluted air ☐

Pure water ☐

Medicines ☐

Drug abuse ☐

Being overwieght ☐

Poster for Healthy Living

Think and do

I keep healthy by ...

. . . .

. . . .

Design a poster and slogan to promote *healthy living*.

© Janet O'Neill, Alan Jones and Roy Purnell

What to do
Answer these questions.

I must always wash my hands before eating food because ...

. . . .

I must always wash my hands after going to the toilet because ...

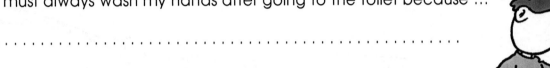

. . . .

I must always use a handkerchief when sneezing because ...

. . . .

Doctors always wash their hands in disinfectant after treating
a patient because ...

. . . .

Doctors always use new needles when giving injections because ...

. . . .

Think and do
Complete this rhyme:

Coughs and sneezes spread **d** . . . .

Micro-organisms

Read

Micro-organisms are living things that can only be seen with a microscope.

Some micro-organisms are helpful. Others are harmful.

Investigate

Dissolve 1 teaspoon of sugar in 150 ml of warm water. Add 1 tablespoon of dried yeast.

1 teaspoon sugar

1 tablespoon dried yeast

600 ml jug

150 ml warm water

Stir well.
Leave for 15 minutes in a warm place.
Draw what happens.

Cross out the incorrect word:
Yeast is a **helpful/harmful** micro-organism.

You could use your yeast to make bread. How? . . . .

. . . .

. . . .

Think and do

Make a list of all the micro-organisms you can think of.
Write if they are helpful or harmful.

. . . .

. . . .

. . . .

Lightning Source UK Ltd.
Milton Keynes UK
UKOW03f0744060115

244067UK00005B/25/P